Blooming

Also by Alexandra Vasiliu

__Healing Words__: A Poetry Collection For Broken Hearts

Blooming

Poems

on Love, Self-Discovery, and Femininity

Alexandra Vasiliu

Stairway Books

Boston

Text copyright © 2019 Alexandra Vasiliu

Cover Image and Illustrations - Ihnatovich Maryia via
www.shutterstock.com

Editing services provided by Chris at
www.hiddengemsbooks.com

**Blooming. Poems on Love, Self-Discovery, and
Femininity** by Alexandra Vasiliu. Boston. Stairway
Books, 2019

ISBN-13: 978-1799121374

To my only one

Contents

Poems

on Love, Self-Discovery, and Femininity

Seeding

BLOOMING

*

When you plant flowers,

you need gentle hands.

When you seed love and happiness,

you need a soft heart.

- *Soft*

*

You took
all of my dreams
and buried them
at the bottom
of the ocean.

Then you left me.

I ran to the shore
and wept
until my tears
became another ocean.
It was
made of my pains,
my failures,

my wounds,

my blood,

my tears,

my cries.

It was an ocean

into which I could dive

and see

the depths of my heart.

"Someday

you will love again.

Someday

you will be loved too,"

the ocean whispered to me.

Those words were

merely a seed,

which I took

and planted

deep in my heart.

Only there

was the seed protected,

growing with

the force of a promise.

- *A Promise Is A Seed*

*

If we could speak

in feelings,

would you, please,

choose only love?

– *Speaking In Feelings*

*

If it rained

kisses,

I would lie down

and open my heart

like a warm

and hungry

earth.

I would like

to nurture my heart

with those invisible seeds

of tenderness.

Then I would wait

to grow.

Only for love.

- *The Seeds Of Tenderness*

*

"Let me kiss your wounds!"
you said to me.

You touched
my broken heart
with your lips.

The walls
of my loneliness
shook.

All of my pains
vanished.

The darkness cleared.

Rivers of light and joy

ran

in every cell

of my body.

"Now let me kiss your seedlings!"

you told me.

And from that moment

my heart tasted

like honey.

- Healing Is A Flower

*

I dreamed of fairy tales
until I met you.
I left everything
and ran to your reality
like seeking refuge
in a castle.
I ran
with my whole heart
clothed in hope,
wishing to live with you
in our own fairy tale.

- Running

*

Let me forever be

a woman

made of

sunlight,

so you can see me

even

in your darkest hours.

- *I Am Your Woman*

*

I would have liked

to see

your heart,

like I saw

the landscape

of a city.

Sometimes

I imagined

your feelings were

busy highways.

I would have liked

to view

your emotions,

growing among worries
like beautiful flowers
amid weeds.

When dark thoughts
started haunting you,
I would have liked
to sit with you and say,
"You will win.
This is just a passing phase."

I would have liked
to help your hopes rise
in the middle of the night
like fearless stars.

I would have liked
to see

your heart,

like I saw

the landscape

of a city.

Maybe it would have been

the easiest way

for me

to win your heart.

- If I Could Have Seen

*

I dream of a beautiful love

like a fresh,

verdant

spring.

A love

which could sing

in my heart,

"You are

my soulmate."

- *The Love That I Dream Of*

*

If the hearts of lovers

had

a distinct hallmark,

then it would be

a seal of light.

- *Harmony*

BLOOMING

*

I will reach

your heart,

no matter how many roads

I must travel,

no matter how many oceans

I must swim,

no matter how many days

I must sigh for your name,

no matter how many nights

I must fall asleep

hungry and thirsty.

I will reach

your heart,

no matter how many obstacles

I must overcome,

no matter how many walls

I must break down,

no matter how many deserts

I must cross,

no matter how many deaths

I must experience.

I will reach

your heart,

no matter how heavy

my longing would weigh,

no matter how much

your absence

would sadden me.

I will reach

your heart,

even if it takes me years

and I become old

like a grandmother's whisper.

One day,

I will.

I promise you.

From that day on,

I will be

the sun of your love.

- Toward Your Heart

*

If you want to run

to a quiet place

at the end

of this world,

just run with me.

If you want to close

your eyes

and dream of love,

just let me

lie down

between your visions.

If you want to be silent

and not say a word,

just make room for me

in your heart

where I can listen to

the music of your emotions.

If you want to stare at the world,

just let me be

your new horizon.

Just let me be with you.

Nothing else.

- Run With Me

*

Forever and ever,

may your heart

be filled

with snowdrops!

Forever and ever,

may your heart

be filled

with light!

Forever and ever,

may your heart

be blessed!

- Forever And Ever

*

If I looked at you
through the window of innocence,

I could see
the other side of your soul,

Where fairies and princes live,
along with your belief in goodness,
honesty and love,

Where you hide
a magical fountain of simplicity
and a wealth of pure joy.

If I looked at you

through the window of innocence,

I could fall in love with

all your childlike secrets.

– Your Secret Self

*

You planted tiny seeds of love

in my heart.

You prayed every morning.

"Let love grow

and spread beauty in all your heart,

in all your feelings,

in all your hopes!

Let love grow!"

One day,

the seeds sprouted

and turned my heart into

a magnificent garden.

– *Your Prayer*

*

Your love reveals the path

to my secret self.

"Come in!

Here is my treasure."

"Let me show you

my hidden flower of innocence

rooted

in my femininity,

in my discreet smiles,

in my untold words,

in my sweetness,

in my poetry,

in my everything.

This is my treasure,

and I want to give it to you."

– The Hidden Flower

BLOOMING

*

Let love be free,

like a fresh morning

in the wilderness.

What bliss!

- *Space For Happiness*

*

The power of love
seems to be descended
from the sun.

It illuminates.

It grows.

It shines.

It gives.

It burns.

It humbles.

It cleanses.

It forgives.

It returns
your heart
to life.

I believe

the power of love

comes from

an incredibly wonderful

place,

one that is

out of this world.

- Love Does Not Come

*

In the beginning,

healing is just a hope,

tiny like a poppy seed.

If you take care of it,

watering its roots,

nurturing its flowers,

then one day

this small seed

will make your heart

bloom.

You will start a new life.

- *The Seeds Of Healing*

BLOOMING

Tonight,

don't tell me sweet words.

Just borrow

the moon's silence for me!

Then, my darling,

go deep inside my heart

and unearth

the maze of my paradise.

Kiss me

and untangle

my twisted paths

not made of

flesh and blood.

At the crack of dawn,

whisper to me softly,

"I am all yours."

- *Just Borrow!*

*

I know

why you turned off

the light.

Your eyes

will become

stars.

- *Your Light*

*

A thousand years
means nothing
to my heart.

I have already waited
a thousand years for you
and my love is the same.

Love outlives time.

- *Love Outlives Time*

*

When I looked deep
into your eyes,
I saw something else.

A sun rose from nowhere
and bade me follow it
until I reached your heart.

Traveling deeper still,
eventually I arrived
at a hidden door
that kept
all your wishes contained.

I pushed the handle.

*

When I was a little girl,

I thought that being beautiful

was something

mixed up with fantasy,

something like

climbing up to the sky,

picking a bunch of stars,

and adding them to my hair.

When I grew up,

I realized

that beauty came from love.

BLOOMING

On that day,

I promised myself,

"One day,

I will meet you.

One day,

your love

will make my heart

so happy

that I will truly be beautiful."

- To Be Beautiful

*

I live for the day
when all the earth
will experience
peace and love
like a newborn experiences
blissful dreams.

- Innocence

*

When love and magic

mingle,

I wear

an evening dress

weaved

with your kisses.

- *My Most Stylish Dress*

*

I swam

through millions of waves

to get to you.

I passed

through millions of moments

to be with you.

When we met,

I was happy like a castaway

reaching dry land.

- Happiness

*

Place the royal crown of love

on my head!

I will wear our magic

like an entire universe.

I am your queen.

You are my king.

Place the royal crown of love

on my head

and let's step in our kingdom!

- *The Royal Crown*

*

Love is more

than a simple feeling.

How else could I explain

that love

has always nourished

my heart

like a heavenly honey?

- *More Than A Simple Feeling*

*

I put a kiss
on your pillow.

In the morning,
it turned into
a butterfly.

- *New Ways To Cherish You*

*

When we reach

the ocean's shore,

we don't hear

the sound of waves.

We just listen to

the music of our hearts.

- The Sound Of Love

*

If you give me a ladder,

I will climb to the top

of your heart.

All your dreams

are chained there.

I will break them free,

one by one,

until I fill up

the sky

with the beauty

of your heart.

- Promise

BLOOMING

I love to dive

in your kisses

like deep waves.

I love to hunt

treasures and pearls

in the depths of your heart.

I always come out

refreshed

from the ocean

of your love.

- *Like A Swimmer*

*

Please,
keep my kiss
in your heart,
like a butterfly
on your palm!

- *My Fragile Breath*

BLOOMING

*

My love,

come home

with the moon

condensed into a gemstone,

put the universe on my finger,

even steal

the whole sky for me,

and I will repaint this wonder

in your heart.

– *Be My Lover*

*

Before our dates,

it always rains raw emotions.

It is a sign.

Maybe it happens

when tenderness

sprouts in our hearts.

– Raw Emotions

*

If we dream together,

our dreams

won't just be dreams.

They will be

our wealth.

- If We Dream Together

*

When I look at you,

I know

how you became free.

You simply said,

"Time doesn't exist

anymore."

You erased it

from your mind.

You didn't want to carry

the burden of time

like Atlas holding

the heavens on his shoulders.

Instead,

you chose love

and counted

every healing word.

You became free.

Love set you free.

– How You Became Free

*

Close your eyes!

Don't open them

until I finish

building a new Taj Mahal for you!

Day and night I will work

to build it

from immaterial things,

but first

I will start

with kindness.

- *A New Taj Mahal*

Growing

*

Wherever there is room

for growth,

there is also room

for love.

Tend beautiful feelings

in your heart's garden.

Let them expand.

No fence is needed

for a good heart.

– No Fence

If someone hurts you,

still leave your heart

open.

This is how the pain will find

an exit.

- *An Exit*

BLOOMING

If I can hear

the flapping wings of butterflies,

believe me,

I can also hear

the footsteps

of your dreams

entering

my heart.

If I can taste

the sweetness of honey,

believe me,

I can also taste

the sweetness

of your love

reaching

deep inside

my heart.

If I can believe

in your love,

I can also believe

in the promise

of your heart

when it says,

"I want to stay

with you

forever."

- *Believe Me!*

BLOOMING

*

If I could sip the rain
drop by drop,
I would rewind time
to my youth.

I would try to win back
my unbroken, brave, and daring
teenage heart.

I would soar again
to the heights of love,
like birds flying,
hugging the sky
with their wings.

If I could sip the rain

drop by drop,

I would try to know

what happiness feels like.

- *My Unbroken Heart*

*

My darling,

after our first date

something magical

happened

to me.

I knew all of our tomorrows

would have

your smile.

- All Of Our Tomorrows

*

If I had to describe

the appearance of your love,

then I would choose

light.

Just light.

- *The Appearance Of Your Love*

*

When you hug me,

I don't see the sky.

I don't touch

the ground anymore.

I just feel

the flowers of hope

growing

in my heart.

- The Flowers Of Hope

*

If you want to go somewhere,
all I ask is
that you take me along.
I will not question
where we will go,
since happiness is not a place,
it is what you make me feel.

- Take Me With You

*

Whenever you look at me,

I feel the beauty of spring

flowing through my body

and enveloping my heart.

It is like getting a gift

every time you look at me.

- Our Romance

*

With you by my side,

I walk the line

between

heaven and life.

After a while,

they fuse

and form a place

where I don't need

to look for happiness

anymore.

- *With You*

*

Please, take your pains,

your wounds,

your tears,

and carry them away

to the end

of the world!

Throw them

in that black abyss

and forget them

for good!

Let them crash

in the darkness!

Let them burn to ashes!

Then,
come back to me,
cuddle up
in my arms
and let's start
all over again!

– *A New Beginning*

*

I can see a path

in your eyes.

It starts at

the bottom of your heart

and goes

through my fears.

This is the path

that opens the door

to my fragile emotions

and makes room

for joy.

This is the path

which carries

your tenderness,

like a river

carries strength

gathered from many springs.

This is the path

flowing down

into my heart

like a waterfall of passion.

I always take

this path

to go home,

to my heart

and to our love.

- *The Path To My Heart*

*

On your lips,

I saw a dreamland.

When I came closer,

you kissed me

until I became

a soft whisper.

– In Heaven

*

When I fell in love,
I didn't fall
into an abyss
or over a cliff.

I just fell for you
like a river flows
into an ocean.

- *Falling In Love*

*

I promise

I will love you

so much

and so deeply

that you will be able

to make peace

with your past.

I promise

I will love you

so much

and so deeply

that you will be healed

from your depression

and anxiety.

I promise

I will love you

so much

and so deeply

that you will fight again

for all the dreams

and all the wishes

of your heart.

- I Promise

*

You asked me
why I love you.

From the millions of reasons,
three came to mind first.
You are
my unbelievable,
my unforgettable,
my unfeigned
soulmate.

– Why?

*

Open your heart
like you would open
a book!

I want to learn
the language
of your heart.
I want to read
everything
about you.
I want to know
all about
your lonely nights,
your wounds,
your desires,

your thoughts,

your dreams expressed

in your smiles.

I want to find

a way

to understand you.

Open your heart

like you would open

a book!

In return,

I want to love you.

- *A Good Reader*

BLOOMING

*

Leave

all the world

at the door.

Turn the key

and stop all the noises.

Please, come in

with a smile on your face

and the whispers of love

on your lips.

Bring flowers home

and shower me

with blooming kisses!

Leave

all the world

at the door!

We won't need it

to be free and happy.

- *Stay With Me*

*

I wish

your body

were transparent,

so I could always see

your heart

beating for me.

- *I Wish...*

*

I miss you so much
every time you leave,
that I gather the air
where you sat down.

I make molds
from our kisses.
I make statues
from our hugs.
I fill up the entire house
with our love.

That is the only way
I can dwell
in your incorporeal arms.

That is the only way

I can remember your touch.

That is the only way

I can feel your sensuality again.

I gather the air

where you sat down,

for I miss you so much

every time you leave.

- Sculptures In The Air

*

You just looked at me
and said
without words,
"I believe in you."
That is how you healed
my soul's wounds.

- *Power*

*

For me,

all the roads to your heart

are one way.

No exit.

This is what

the hunger for love

means.

- *All The Roads*

*

Your caresses are like sailboats

that save my heart

from the sea of darkness

and take it

to paradise.

- *To Paradise*

*

Tonight,

let your hair down!

Cover me

with your soft tresses!

I don't need to see

anything.

I just want to feel

the heat of our hugs

and follow our hearts

in their flight

for a new home.

- Tonight

*

We melt in love
like honey dissolves in milk.

We became one.
Sharing only one heart.

- *What A Fresh Feeling!*

*

If I could live

in a wonderful palace,

I would choose a palace

not made of gold,

silver, or marble.

I would love to live in a palace

made of our heartbeats

with moonbeams tangled in our hair.

I would love to live

like your queen,

and not like an ordinary woman.

- *A Palace*

*

I was afraid
I wouldn't find you
in this world.

I was afraid
that my dreams
would remain locked forever
in my heart.
Like a hidden treasure.

When we met,
you released
my emotions
like captive birds
from their cages.

It was like

your love

gave birth to me.

Just to be your woman,

I was reborn.

- Free For Good

*

You can get so deep

under my skin,

like an archaeologist

looking for buried treasure.

- An Archaeologist

BLOOMING

When I think of you,

I can see

another sun rising

in the sky.

- *Hope*

*

In the sandglass
of the world,
I can see lovers
hugging.

I know
they are the only ones
who can cease
the flow of time.

- *The Majesty of Love*

BLOOMING

*

"Let me create poetry

in you,"

you told me.

You came close,

opened the door to my feelings,

and cleaned up

my heart's dark walls.

You raised

tiny stars

in my sky.

You planted

seeds of hope

in my feelings.

Eventually,
my heart bloomed.

Poetry
was
everywhere.

- *Poetry In You*

*

With your breath

close to my ear,

I

always

measure

the distance

from Earth to heaven.

- From Earth To Heaven

*

Sometimes

there is so much sadness

in your eyes,

that when I touch

your heart

I can feel

your scars.

- *In Your Eyes*

Blooming

*

If flowers can bloom,
so can your feelings.

If a caterpillar can turn
into a butterfly,
so can your heart.

Just bloom.

- Bloom

*

Let's learn the alphabet of love
without saying a word,
without writing a letter,
without drawing a line!

All we need to do
is find the thread
that weaves our feelings
with miracles.

"H is for *heart."*

"E is for *eyes of love."*

"A is for *astonishment."*

"R is for *remember."*

"T is for *together."*

- The Alphabet Of Love

*

When I was a child,

I held a few sunrays

and some sand

within my grasp.

When I grew up,

I discarded the grains

because flowers don't grow

in the sand.

But I kept the sun,

because I wanted to bloom

one day.

- *Only The Sun*

*

All the buses,

all the people,

all the chances,

all the sorrows,

all the sunsets,

and all the days

of our lives

passed us by.

Eventually, even eternity

passed us by.

Yet, we are still together.

- *After Everything*

*

We have spent our lives

weaving the magic

of our hearts.

Nothing else

seemed more essential.

- *Weaving Our Magic*

BLOOMING

*

Let me be free in your love

like an eagle soaring

in the sky!

Let me be free in your love

like sunrays dancing

in Spring's air!

Let me be free in your love

like a seedling

longing to grow

and bloom in your arms!

- Freedom

BLOOMING

Our words are not

just letters

following other letters.

Our words create

an awesome relationship

between the alphabet of your heart

and the alphabet of my heart;

between your desire to bloom

and my desire to bloom.

Our words illustrate

the intimate dance

between your hopes

and my hopes.

Our sweet words
build magical bridges
between your heart
and my heart,
so your life and my life
can be as one.

- Our Relationship

*

In love we do everything

that is

essential,

eternal,

blissful,

meaningful,

and wise.

In love we do everything,

even in those days

when we stay home

and do nothing at all.

- *What We Do*

*

We'll love each other
until the end of days.

We'll love each other
until the end of time.

We'll love each other
until the end of the world.

We'll love each other
until the end
of everything we know.

We'll love each other
until the end of our last words.

We'll love each other.

It is a promise.

- We'll Love Each Other

*

Hug me,

let all my dreams be bared.

Butterflies are already flying

in my secret garden,

where there is still time

to embrace the moon

and kiss the skin

of this magical night.

Hug me,

we are so free in love

I cannot hold this truth

without tears

in my eyes.

Hug me,

there is still time

to make the flames of our souls

dance

gently

in the moonlight.

- Hug Me

*

Someone once told me,

"You will recognize

true love

when your heart

is able to speak

a totally different language."

"What language?"

"The language of harmony."

And now,

my love,

I have to tell you,

when we are together,

BLOOMING

I always hear
my heart speaking
this language.

- *A Wise Word*

*

I would like to have

a transparent body,

so you can see through me

like a clear window.

No secrets.

Just my heart dancing

to your heart's music.

I would like you to have

a transparent body too,

just like the air.

I could hug you

whenever I want

and believe me,

I always do.

I would like

both of us

to be transparent,

so we could always see

each other.

Without walls.

Without restrictions.

Without secrets.

– *Without Barriers*

*

Let your dreams be free!

Let all your thoughts

collapse

at the night's feet

like cast-off clothes!

Lay your heart

on my palm,

like a dewdrop on a leaf.

Kiss me slowly.

We will have enough time

to melt into the moon's light.

- *Nudity*

*

In your arms, I bloom

like a cherry tree,

all the branches

covered

with raw emotions.

- *Like A Cherry Tree*

*

When the end of the world

comes,

I will wear the dress

you gave me.

I want to welcome

eternity

through your love.

- *This Is My Promise*

*

Tick-tock!
Tick-tock!

"Is it true
that time is passing
for us too?"
I asked you.

Tick-tock!
Tick-tock!

"No, my darling.
We just hear the echoes of time."

Tick-tock!

Tick-tock!

"We are far away,

eternally falling in love."

- A Special Universe

*

I waited for you
an entire afternoon,
until the sun fell asleep
on the branches
of a flowering tree.

When you arrived,
you became
my sun.

– *Waiting For You*

*

You entered my heart
a very long time ago.
You had a key.
A magic key.

"Where did you get this key?"
I asked you.

"From the light
of our kiss."

- *The Magic Key*

*

We opened our arms
to hug
one another.

Our hearts bonded
as we listened to
the beautiful silence
that seemed to whisper,
"Your love feels
like home."

- *Always At Home*

BLOOMING

I yearned for you,

long before I met you.

I knew

you were somewhere

in this big, lonely world.

I knew

you waited for me

and needed to

give me

your love,

your heart,

your life.

I looked for you

everywhere

in this world.

But I didn't find you.

Nobody knew

where you lived.

I yearned for you

so deeply

and desperately.

One day,

I saw the sunrays

smiling at me

with the eyes

of a handsome man.

It was you.

The perfume of spring

filled my whole heart.

- Eventually I Found You

*

When I sleep,

my heart still dreams of you,

because love

knows no rest.

– Love Never Sleeps

*

Whenever I say "you,"
I think of
joy,
for you are the true joy
of my heart.

A joy
like a spring
running through the fields
of my heart.

A joy
like the flowering feelings
that burst into my soul
when I see you.

A joy

that whispers

in my heart,

"I was meant

to be yours."

- *I Think Of Joy*

*

Lovers are always mysterious,
like the face
of the moon.

– Secrets

BLOOMING

*

My friends asked me

what it felt like

to be in love with you.

I couldn't find

the appropriate words

to describe my happiness.

Instead I painted

millions of rivers flowing

from my heart to yours.

- *In Love*

*

I always wanted

to live

in a place

where it was eternally spring.

I traveled

all around

the world

to discover

that bright,

wonderful

place.

One day,

I met you

and I found

in your heart

the bright,

wonderful

place,

where it is eternally spring.

- A Place Like Spring

*

I feel so free loving you,

like a bird

whose nest

is in the sky's arms.

- *My Nest*

BLOOMING

*

Sometimes

I would like

to gather sunrays,

braid them,

and make

a golden hammock.

I would sleep there

all summer long,

while a soft wind

would whisper

your name.

- *Sleeping In Your Arms*

*

I have loved you
from the very beginning,
before all the centuries,
before all the worlds,
before all the languages.

I have loved you
before I had a body
or a name.

I have loved you
before I knew
what love or life meant.

BLOOMING

I have loved you
before my hungry heart
roamed this world
looking for you.

I have loved you
before our first date,
before our first laugh,
before our first kiss.

I have loved you
before all your loving declarations,
before all your dreams
of a life together.

I have loved you

before my passion
burned like fire,
before my longing woke up
like a powerful king.

I have loved you so much
from the very beginning.

And when you came into my life,
I just knew
I was ready to give you
my trust,
my love,
my heart,
my everything.

- From The Very Beginning

BLOOMING

*

You have brought me flowers
since the first time we met.
Flowers that smelled so sweet -
I thought
perhaps they came
from heaven.

Day after day
you gave me so many flowers
until there was no more room
in my house.

Eventually I put them
in every corner of my heart,

in my smile,

in my hair,

in my eyes,

in my whispers,

in my emotions,

in my dreams.

One morning

I woke up realizing

I had become

entirely

your flower.

- *Your Flower*

*

Only when I shut out

the noise of this world,

can I listen

to the music

of your heart.

- *So Happy To Be With You*

*

If I dream of you

from the depths of my heart,

I will not wake up

in the morning.

I will keep living in my dream

like a baby in a warm womb.

And if someday I wake up,

I will have one dream.

To live

for your love.

- Dreaming Of You

BLOOMING

*

Sometimes
when I look into your eyes,
I can see a road
calling me.

I tread
the depths
of your irises
and I start walking.

I find the form of my body,
imprinted on the sheets
of last night's dream.

I move on.

I keep walking.

I see shadows and lights
displayed all over your heart.

"Where do these shadows
come from?"
"These are the regrets
that sometimes I hurt you."
"And the lights?"
"These are our kisses."

"Have I ever told you
why you are so magical to me?"

- *I Keep Walking In Your Heart*

*

My love,

you

are so close

to me

that you can see

my dreams.

- *No Borders*

*

Your longing follows my heart
like shadow follows light.
We can never be separated.

- *You Miss Me*

*

Do you know

I can read

about our love

in all the poems

written

in this world?

- *One Language*

*

When I miss you,

I write your name

on the wind's wings,

and send it

throughout the world.

I want to hear your name

from every corner

of this world.

Like an echo.

"My love,

my love."

- *Your Name*

*

If this world were

a world of caresses,

we could see

one another

with hungry fingers.

- *The World Of Caresses*

*

Your smile melts

all the icebergs of my world,

destroys

all the walls of my past,

cleanses

all the darkness of my soul,

and heals

all the cracks of my heart.

Only your smile.

- *All The Icebergs*

*

I know I am a star,

caught in the thicket

of your dreams,

and you are a soft morning light

scattering my fears,

but we can still make

a new sky

out of our crazy desires.

– Lovers

*

After falling in love,

we lived on the moon.

Beyond worries

and sorrows.

We ate

wonders and miracles

and drank

magic and promises.

Oh, life was so good for us

after falling in love!

We innocently lived on the moon.

- *On The Moon*

BLOOMING

*

Let me write
about our love.

The more I write to you,
the more I can hear
your heart
beating in the body
of my poem.

The more I write to you,
the more I can feel
your arms
hugging my dreams
to your chest.

Let me write to you,
so I can make a home
in your heart
through words
and emotions.

- Letters To You

BLOOMING

*

The waves always return

to my arms,

and so does your longing for me.

The sun always ascends

in the sky

of my heart,

and so does your longing for me.

The wind always hugs me,

and so does your longing for me.

The moon always looks at me,

and so does your longing for me.

The spring always rejoices me,
and so does your longing for me.

The winter always cuddles
my heart,
and so does your longing for me.

Everything treasures me,
and so does your whole heart.

- *Magnetic*

*

Of all the gifts

you gave me,

I most treasure

the spring that awakens

my dreams,

the sun that warms up

my heart,

and the flowers you planted

with your healing words.

- *Of All The Gifts*

*

I would like to live

forever

in one word

and that word would be

"love."

- *One Word*

BLOOMING

*

Every day

we go to

the same beach

and listen to

the same music

of the ocean's waves.

But every day

the waves of our hearts

sing a different song.

- *A Different Melody*

*

When you smile,

all the flowers

in this world

start

blooming.

When you smile,

all the stars

in the sky

start

shining.

When you smile,

all the feelings

I missed

come

into my heart

and promise me

an endless

spring

with you.

- *All In This World*

*

Your love is a breeze.

So fresh,

so soft,

so cheerful,

that all I want

is

to close my eyes

and feel

your touch.

- A Breeze

*

Blessed are your glimpses
that shower me with love.

Blessed are your kisses
that bring back the memory
of our first date.

Blessed are your thoughts
that save me
from waves of sorrows.

Blessed are your healing words
that mend the cracks
of my broken heart.

Blessed are you,

my love,

who were destined

to love me.

Blessed are we,

for we belong

to one another.

– Blessed Are You

BLOOMING

*

If lovers don't need

all the words in the world

to understand one another,

then there are two possibilities:

either not all the words in this world

lead to love,

or not all the words in this world

hold the mystery of love.

Regardless, I choose not to use

all the words.

Lovers don't need them.

– All The Words

*

Since we fell in love,

time has stopped.

Only our hearts grew

bigger and bigger.

Only our hearts conquered

border after border,

until they became

our kingdom

on Earth.

- Since We Fell In Love

*

Where is the Earth
when I am
with you?

I don't see flowers,
butterflies, or sunrays,
but I can feel them all,
in my heart.
Like a secret dance.

Where is the Earth

when I am

with you?

I don't see anything

other than your heart.

You are my mirror.

Where is the Earth

when we are flying hand in hand

toward happiness?

Together

we are a whole world.

- Where Is The Earth?

*

Lovers are blessed people,

for they can treasure

the harmony of stillness.

— *The Truth Of Love*

*

If longing were an invisible chisel,

then I would carve out

all the painful moments

when I was alone

and waited for you

to become part of my life.

If longing were an invisible chisel,

then I would carve out

all the painful moments

when I needed you most

to comfort my heart,

to make me smile after a tough day,

and to protect

my innocent dreams.

BLOOMING

If longing were an invisible chisel,

then I would carve out

all the painful moments

when I searched for you,

but never knew

who you were

or where you lived.

If longing were an invisible chisel,

then I would carve out

all the painful moments

when I sat down

with my phone

and never found someone

with a loving heart

to call.

If longing were an invisible chisel,

then I would carve out

all the painful moments

when I cried

in the middle of the night

wondering

where you were

in this world,

what you looked like,

and what your name was

so I could whisper it

or hold it

in my thoughts.

Oh, I would carve out

all these painful moments.

Then I would fashion them

into birds

and let them fly

to the edge of the earth,

never again to be seen.

- *Special Birds*

*

Sometimes

my heart grows arms

that lift you above

the worries of this world,

somewhere you can

dance with the sun.

- Dancing With The Sun

BLOOMING

*

For you,

I would put our best memories

on my lap,

like a ball of wool.

I would unravel them

slowly, slowly,

just to live our story again.

- Our Best Memories

*

Your heart

is

a pearl

in my hands.

- *Totally Precious*

*

Sleep peacefully

and let me kiss your eyelids.

I yearn

to lose myself in them.

When you open your eyes,

the first miracle you will see

will be me.

- *Let Me Kiss You*

*

So what

if it is getting dark?

Your love is always

my sun.

- So What?

*

After I fell in love with you,

my heart grew wings

and I waited to fly with you.

Day and night,

I wanted you to show me

your paradise.

Day and night,

I imagined how you could invite me.

"Come, hurry up,

I will open

my little paradise for you.

Come, stay with me forever."

- *Day And Night*

*

If I look deeply

at the heart

of some words,

I can see

they know not death.

Like love.

Love is an immortal word.

- *Some Words*

*

I wish

I could be

all four seasons

for you,

if you wanted to spend

your entire life

with me.

- *All The Seasons*

*

There are many ways
to see you,
when I merely close
my eyes.

I can see you
with my mouth
when my lips crave
your heart.

I can see you
with my hands
when my fingers run
over your body.

I can see you

with my ears

when I dive into

your whispers

and hear the songs

of your love.

There are many ways

to see you,

when I merely close

my eyes.

– *To See You*

*

Cover me
with your touch.
Wrap my bare skin
in moonbeams
that glow and glitter
like your soft kisses.

- *Cover Me!*

*

I made my home of you
to worship
your heart.

Home is my love for you
and your love for me.

Home is your name
on my tongue,
your soft kisses
on my neck.

Home is my footsteps
following your wishes.

Home is my arms
gently wrapped around
your waist.

Home is my love for you
and your love for me.

Home is you
and your heart's invisible castle
that can't be ruined.

Home is me
and the power of my love
beating
in my flesh
and in my blood.

Home is you and me.

Home is love,

and this is why

I made my home of you.

- *You Are My Home*

*

If I could build

something sturdy

in this world,

something that wouldn't crash,

melt,

or rust,

then I would make a bridge

from my heart to yours.

I would shape this bridge

out of our beliefs and promises,

out of our feelings and desires.

I would frame it with magic,

so only you and I could see it.

And whenever the world hurt us

or made us lose

the power of dreaming,

we would take a walk

over this bridge

and win back

our strength.

- Build A Bridge!

*

I don't want

to write poems for you.

I just want to give birth

to the feelings

you awaken

in my soul;

to give

a beautiful body

to the words

I treasure

in my heart for you.

- *My Feelings For You*

BLOOMING

I am a seedling

waiting to grow

in your heart.

I am a ripe fruit

waiting to be consumed

by your lips.

I am a flock of seagulls

looking for the land

of your arms.

I am a raindrop

lost in the desert

of this world,

wishing to rest
on the petals
of your feelings.

I am a cherry tree
fully blooming
in your secret paradise.

- You and I

BLOOMING

*

I am made of jewels
like love is made
of heaven's air.

I am made of joy
like flower fields are made
of sun and wilderness.

I am made of mysteries
like galaxies are made
of secrets and majesty.

I am made of sky
like a love song is made
of intangible beauty.

I am made of weaknesses
and strengths
like life is made
of endings and births.

I am made for you
like everything else
that is wonderful and
fragile, yet timeless.
This is why
I want to bloom
only for you.

- I Am Made

Dear Reader

Thank you for reading my poems. I hope they have resonated with you.

If you enjoyed this poetry book, the best way to show your appreciation is to spread the word. So please take a moment and leave a short review at the retailer's site where you purchased it.

And if you haven't already read *Healing Words*, my empowering poetry book for broken hearts, no worries, discover it now and let your heart be healed. Thank you for allowing me the privilege to nourish your heart with inspirational poems. I am grateful beyond words.

About The Author

Alexandra Vasiliu is an award-winning poet. As far back as she can remember, she has had a rich imagination. She began composing poems at the age of 8. Of particular interest were figures of speech, which lent itself well to writing poetry. Alexandra's love of reading and writing led her to the wonderful world of books. She earned a PhD in Medieval Literature from Bucharest University, editing many novels in this genre.

Alexandra grew up in Romania and currently lives in Massachusetts with her family. When she is not writing,

Alexandra is a busy wife and mother who can't imagine her life without laughter and hugs. She is a dreamer, coffee fiend, happy traveler, and a lighthearted optimist.

Find out more at her blog www.alexandravasiliu.net and get a beautiful selection of her inspirational poems. Keep in touch with her on social media:

www.pinterest.com/AlVasiliuWriter/

www.instagram.com/alexandravasiliuwriter/

www.facebook.com/AlexandraVasiliuWriter

Made in the USA
Coppell, TX
05 January 2021